Three midc
week off. There is nothing original about this journey and the cliché is not lost in the excitement. The
opportunity to escape on a bike is one which has
been seized by many and enjoyed by almost all.

This memoir just one person's thoughts as the great
British roads rolled beneath him, the scenery
flashed before him, and the world was stopped
from passing him by.

An honest account of a fantastic week spent alone
with friends.

Front Cover
Dom on Wide Glide, Hardknott Pass, Cumbrian Mountains

Back Cover
The three bikes overlooking the A82, West Highlands, Scotland

ISBN: 978-1-4092-8025-5
Copyright: © 2008 Standard Copyright License
Language: English
Country: United Kingdom
Version: 3

Acknowledgements

Emma
Chris and Paul

Contents

A Beginning

I am not really sure how stress works; if it is something which happens upon us overnight or as a cumulative effect. I am more inclined towards the latter, but as I have no medical or psychological education nor amateur understanding, it is probably better for me not to venture any form of formal diagnosis. I can say, however, that during a five year period I left a comfortable corporate life, presided over the birth of three businesses, the death of one, made many thousands of pounds and had a few of them stolen along with most of my ability to trust. I have had the great honour to watch two wonderful children grow in the image of a serene and beautiful mother. Risked everything and lost most of it, won it back through hard work and given heart, soul and a few pounds of flesh in the process.

None of this is remarkable or unique. If you are in your mid forties, living and working in the United Kingdom, then the last paragraph could as easily describe your life as mine. The effect it was all starting to have on me, however, was neither pleasant for me nor those around me. The spiral of behaviour was both compelling and revolting.

The recognised fascination with the pursuance of wealth, recognition and all the trappings is both addictive and destructive. Like a drug, the success (not the money) of winning contracts, delivering against a target, being known as the best, both buoys and weighs with equal bearing. To stop and spend time with the family is clearly the most logical thing to do, but the next contract is such a compliment, and it's only six more months, and I'll only be away three nights a week.....

Meanwhile the lifestyle ramps up a notch.

A Beginning

Time together must be '*quality time*', skiing in Canada replaces skiing in France, which replaced Centre Parcs, which replaced a cottage in Wales, sitting around the table playing Scrabble. Summer in the Maldives, which replaced Greece, which replaced France which replaced every weekend on Saunton Sands sleeping in a shitty old camper, laughing. Now I can't stop, I can't afford to.

We agreed we would start a family when we were earning £15k pa, the rest is history.

Again I don't know how stress works, accept that it seems to come when it shouldn't. Money was not a problem, work was plentiful, kids were wonderful and the house was nearly paid for. I am sure it has everything to do with time. I didn't have time for my children, I didn't have time for my wife and I didn't have time for myself.

This piece/book describes a very obvious journey, the cliché and predictability of three Western European men in the 21st century choosing such a journey is 'blindingly obvious'. What is important is that nobody embarked upon the journey with any metaphysical objective or great quest but simply to have a bit of a giggle.

Chris and I have been friends since university, the kind of friends that can, and do, argue about anything. In fact so close that at times we could argue with the hatred and venom that would only usually be reserved for siblings.

Chris makes his living as a freelance journalist and manages to combine, on the face of it at least, a successful journalistic career with being an attentive father who is home more than he is away, one of the very many things I envied in the people around me on this journey. Chris and I met in the College Bar in 1985. I have no clearly defined memory of our first encounter, but what was clear was that we both had the good sense to 'get involved' in Students Union business as early as possible in our educational careers. We had both studied Animal Farm at school and knew that all students should be equal; we simply aspired to the trough. The strategy paid off for both of us, within days we were both working a couple of nights a week behind the bar and on door security for every major social event. This rapidly developed into roles within the Union and Social Committee. These roles carrying a guaranteed pick of the prime jobs and free access to all events, i.e. money and a free pass! Whilst always advocating the Orwellian precept of '*equality*'. Darwin's '*survival of the fittest*' was far more apt.

Over several years Chris and I had discussed the desire to obtain motorbikes and ride somewhere,

A Beginning

anywhere. In truth the plan had hatched when we had, in 1989, hitched to Pamplona for the Fiesta de San Fermin (something of a Hemmingway pilgrimage), more commonly referred to as the Bull Run. During this excursion we had remarked on how good it would be to do the trip on bikes. Since then occasionally dredging up the suggestion, with no great conviction. Not until early 2006, when we vowed to do the trip that summer. Sadly I let Chris down, as badly as one could let anyone down, giving him only one week's notice of my failure to attend, "pressure of work". Most people would have responded badly, not Chris, his plans changed and within days he was en-route to the Dolomites on his trusty Africa Twin, alone. I worked. Already my mental state was such that I would have chewed on such a let-down until it became sour and unpalatable, Chris simply insisted that I promise to organise my diary better for the following year.

Deeply troubled by my treatment of him, I made damn sure that my diary was clear for the following year. Planning consisted of conversations over fabulous Pizzas and Indian Takeaways at Chris's place in South East London whenever I was working in London, which in late 2006 and early 2007 was often. Plans ranged from San Fermin, to Denmark and Norway via Amsterdam. Circumnavigating France was another suggestion, it was during this session that we realised how little we knew about our own country. We hit upon riding the Four Compass Points of the United Kingdom mainland. I called it the Four Corners, which of course, in the UK, it isn't.

As previously stated, this was simply a boys' trip, nothing more. Four objectives to meet one very clearly defined goal, underwritten by a desire to have fun riding our bikes, seeing our country and being on the kind of trip we should have done in our twenties.

Once decided and the dates set we gently geared our planning and thinking towards our goal. In the months that followed many people expressed an interest in participating. Some even made definite commitments. Routes were planned, equipment begged, borrowed, purchased and, in one case, stolen (my son's camping stove).

The journey was planned for June and in the preceding months the number of potential participants had risen from two to nine and back to three. Each predictably slipping away as time marched on. This is no criticism of the individuals. After all it was only twelve months earlier that I had broken my promise to Chris to join him on the San Fermin ride. The 'Pressure of Work' imperative is compelling and totally unavoidable... regardless of what the Satellite TV Nannies would have us all believe

A Beginning

as they trot out the predictable criticisms of fathers whose work takes them away and women who don't have time to show little Tarquin how to turn pots and make '*quiche*'. Paying the mortgage turns us into terrible parents. Catch 22.

The third player was Paul. We had only met a few times. Our boys are school buddies. Front gate and party doorstep conversations had somehow got onto the subject of bikes and the trip itself. Conversations between mums at the school gate seem to focus very much on the children but with dads it's different, it seems to be a great opportunity for demonstrating that we still have the bachelor freedoms, we still have toys and we still use them. Either that or we talk about how we are working too hard and are too tired to do anything. However we got to the subject of the Four Corners Tour, Paul was locked in and very welcome. A confident but not overbearing man, Paul runs his own business, self assured, softly spoken and always smiling. I also got the impression that Paul didn't suffer fools gladly, if at all… On balance Paul was far more the listener. A trait I often envy when I am fortunate enough to encounter it, not least because I wish I could hold my own tongue a little more than I do. Paul, like Chris, also managed to organise his working life from home. This allowed him time with his family. It was clear that once Paul had said he was coming, this was treated as his word, and in true British spirit, his bond.

The Ride

The Bikes and Riders

Three more different stallions could not have been chosen to carry this 123 year old trio into the unknown.

Paul rode a 20 year old classic Kawasaki GPZ900cc. It should be noted that the GPZ had a very lack lustre appearance but was obviously loved and nurtured. This was reassuring as it was obvious that Paul had dismantled and reassembled this machine on many occasions; moreover he clearly knew how engines worked. His command going far beyond my rudimentary understanding of the internal combustion engine, gleaned from the Encyclopaedia Britannica (children's edition). The GPZ was fast, made for good surfaces, winding roads and the kind of quick, fun riding we were aiming for. To the trained eye this was a classic, a little gem.

Chris was on the ultimate all-rounder: the Honda Africa Twin 750cc. There was nothing this bike would not do, designed for the Paris Dakar run. About the same age as the GPZ, Chris' bike was nowhere near as attractive but without a doubt the best equipped bike on the tour. It had something of the Camel Land Rover about it…. Dangerously close to becoming what bikers refer to as a '*Rat Bike*', Chris had attached every possible 'bit' and 'bob'. Panniers had been made by a friend; racks cut and welded to Chris' specification. Power outlets were abundant, Satellite Navigation, Short Wave and FM radio transmitter and receiver, hands free telephone, MP3 player, bags securely attached from every available anchor point and in all that, room for Chris. We were seeing this bike in the middle of its evolution, not fully grown. I dare not say fully grown.

My own bike an 11 year old Harley Davidson FXDWG 1340cc (otherwise referred to as a *Dyna Wide Glide*). Although she had the biggest engine, this bike was by far the least suited to the journey weighing in at 270kgs (dry and un-laden). Well loved by me and its previous owner, the *Wide Glide* was nothing if not comfortable. The saddle more closely related to a leather Chesterfield than anything the others would have to endure. This said she was designed for American roads, big American roads, few turns and not having to follow and keep up with leaner, fitter more nimble machines. So it's muscular advantage clearly outweighed by its sheer bulk. But for the next few weeks at least this machine was to be my home.

So three bikes; each suited to a completely different set of riding conditions. Paul it turns out is an ex-instructor. Careful, considerate and very capable, once on his bike they became one. Smooth riding with every move appearing to be well planned and thought out. Nothing happened without due warning. Chris rides in London everyday. He is quick thinking, brilliant on this bike and awesome at seeing a gap and getting through it. Inspirational to watch. Like every London based dispatch rider (clearly Chris' alter-ego) he had also gone more than slightly insane, so following him too closely was totally out of the question, though this lesson would have to be learned the hard way. My own approach was extremely tense when riding in the wet but more relaxed as conditions improved. The *Wide Glide* and I had still to get to know each other fully. By far the least experienced of the group, I need to be very careful when dishing out any form of criticism. I had masses to learn from these guys and was looking forward to the prospect. In fact I was very nervous about my abilities on the bike which resulted in an intangible reserve about the entire trip.

The Four Corners

April and May 2007 were record breakers with, according to the weather men, every formal record being tumbled as the months progressed. Predictably we were all highly enthusiastic for a hot June. How naïve.

With June came rain, rain that was not to stop until the middle of August. Rain that would, in the same way as April and May, re-write the record books, flooding in Somerset, flooding in Gloucestershire, damns breaking in Yorkshire and so on.

The Liquorice Road

We had decided to start our ride in the West Country, The Lizard is the most southerly tip of the UK mainland, not Land's End as is popularly believed. There are only a few miles between the two but The Lizard is a far less frequented place. Paul and I live in the West Country (North Somerset), so by starting here we could then easily ride up the Western side of the UK and back down the East (the theory was magically simple). This would be the only part of the trip that would involve us having to double back on ourselves though we would make all efforts not to retrace any roads. In fact some of the rules we would try and maintain throughout were:

Avoid retracing our tracks
Avoid using Motorways
Camp out as much as possible

The Ride

We had 10 days!

This would be an absolute doddle!

Friday 15th June 2007
Day 1

Like all of the best laid plans the disintegration set in early. It had been raining solidly for a week, alternating between a fine penetrative mist and horizontal sheets of water. Big rain, with big rain-drops! The BBC weather service showed rain right across the UK with one bright dry area, the West Highlands. We were not due in the West Highlands until Monday 18th, corresponding, according to the BBC, with the arrival of the rain.

Chris lives in Lewisham in South East London. He had set off shortly after dropping his daughter at school. He needed to ride through the centre of London and then get onto the Motorway (the mo-torway rule did not apply until we were all

The Ride

together) to ride the 135 miles to meet Paul and me. Fitted with his new metal panniers the Africa Twin was nearly as wide as a small car, so progress across London must have been frustratingly slow, especially for Chris. Once on the Motorway he should have been with us in an hour and a half. The rain and traffic conspired against us all, the journey taking him a total of 4 hours.

As we drank tea at my house the rain continued to fall, the water on the patio reached over two inches in depth. This became the scene of a definitive conversation, a conversation that had the potential to change the entire week. "Have you got your passport"? My thinking was very simple, we could ride the 100 miles to Plymouth and get a ferry to Santander in northern Spain and spend the rest of the week riding back. Chris looked at me coldly, still shivering from his ordeal. He gazed upon me as though I had just killed his sister's puppy, slowly, in front of her. "That would have been a good idea 5 hours ago". "OK, no worries, just a thought". We moved on quickly.

The rains subsided and light blazed temporarily through the clouds. A 5 mile ride over to Paul's place where he was waiting patiently. Introductions were made briefly and we set off at 15:00. More than half of the day lost to the weather. The original plan was to get to The Lizard by the end of the first day. Whilst we were setting off with this in mind, it was clearly a stretch objective. For the next 100 miles it rained on and off but not with any great vigour. We avoided motorway traffic sticking to the A38 and then the A30. Even on these big roads progress was painfully slow. Strangely the June warmth remained so we were wet and warm, already after 3 hours of riding my leathers were wet through, my waterproofs were simply not working. The plan to get to the Lizard was quickly shelved in favour of a warm place to stop for the night.

After Exeter we headed for the Tolkienesk landscape of Dartmoor. Dank mist pillowing over the hills and through the trees, the roads winding tightly up and down under arches of foliage. Trunks covered in deep green moss betraying the fact that this place spends many months a year shrouded in a dense mist. I hate riding in wet weather, even more than this the *Wide Glide* hates slow tight corners especially when wet. If ever I was going to drop the bike it would be here.

A strange thing happens when you get nervous riding. Your shoulders tighten and you start to concentrate on the road just in front of the bike, looking down for hazards, concentrating on the surface and not the wider road itself, your view and vista become narrowed, you get 'tunnel vision'. On a Harley this is suicidal behaviour, Harleys don't like corners at the best of times. The only way to ride in these conditions is to keep your head up, relax and look well ahead. The golden rule is look where you want to go and the bike will follow. If you look down at the road, that is where you will end up. The problem is that as soon as you get nervous the default behaviour is to concentrate on where you think the biggest risk is, in this case the wet road directly in front of the front wheel.

The parallel with my own life was staggering and obvious. On a daily basis I struggled to identify my goals, where did I want to be and choosing the right line. Keeping relaxed and your head up is the only way to see all of the hazards, all of the potential scenarios. By doing this you quickly recognise if you have taken a wrong turn, you can quickly and safely make corrections. This logic holds strong for family life, friendships and career along with their inevitable combination. Lose the wider picture and drop the bike, drop the bike and do untold damage, waste time, resource and enthusiasm getting back to square one.

I forced myself to look up, retraining myself to ride in a completely different way. I straightened up and looked ahead, deliberately spotting the apex of each bend well in advance. Counter steering the bike and religiously following the lines that Paul was taking in front of me. He knew what he was doing, why would I be so stupid as not to follow his lead. He in turn followed Chris who knew the road.

As the road ejected us from the belly of the forest and onto the high moors the sky allowed a few shafts of brilliant white light to pierce through the jet black clouds, electric silver linings betraying what was hidden above the dark morass of sky we had become so used to. I could scarcely contain the joy and relief; I was exhausted by the last 20 miles of riding. Forcing myself to see the road differently, changing my style completely and exercising a degree of humility which, to be frank, was extremely uncomfortable. I didn't know whether to be overjoyed of appalled. I chose the former.

Princetown appeared before us with the Dartmoor Prison to our right. One of my French ancestors had spent time there during the Napoleonic Wars…. I considered for a moment that perhaps the choices we were making on a daily basis were not perhaps as foolish as they could be. Chris astutely decided to cut the days riding objective at the Plume of Feathers. We pulled in and charged for the bar. Yes there was accommodation, the bunk house was available and at £10 each per night. At these prices there was no way we were going to camp. Chris was clearly a little disappointed at this decision but the lure of a pint or three of Tinners

and a hot meal soon persuaded him otherwise, and
at least we were dry and could dry our things.

Princetown is a very small town in the middle of
one of England's wildernesses; one could easily
have been mistaken for thinking our first night
would be spent in a deserted pub, being stared at by
disparaging locals with weathered hands, gruff
voices and wearing battered tweed sports jackets
discarded many years previously by, "his Lord-
ship". Actually this could not have been further
from the truth. The evening was everything it
should be, plenty of good banter and conversations
with people on the tables around us. The place
filled with teenagers and Venture Scout instructors,
it turned out that despite the weather and severe
weather warnings, these guys were even more insane than us. They were planning to spend the next
three days training for Ten Tors[1] and Duke of Edinburgh events by Camping out and Orienteering
their way through the entire weekend. Their enthusiasm was infectious. These kids were not hanging
out on corners, not tempting ASBOS, they were not
the kind of teenagers that make the 6pm news or
instil fear and loathing. These were another group,
a forgotten youth, they were the respectful, enthu-

---

[1] Ten Tors is an annual orienteering and survival event
which takes place on Dartmoor, involving people of all
ages. The event carries significant risk to life in under-
taken lightly

siastic, interesting, challenging youth. It was great to just sit in the room and listen to the buzz.

An excellent Steak and Ale pie chased down by three pints of Tinners, I was ready for my bed.

As well as camping, some of the Duke of Edinburgh trainees were occupying the same bunkhouse as us, ten to be precise. My heart sank, I was convinced that ten teenagers in one room would result in a night with no sleep for us, their neighbours, and we had a huge day of riding ahead of us. Not so, this forgotten youth. We slept undisturbed; the night was event free and I enjoyed a deep sleep with no dreams. A week earlier and I would have been appalled to see a bedroom with 10 beds (five bunks) and not enough room for two to pass between them.

The Ride

There was no en-suite, no mini bar, the room service phone had clearly been omitted, I couldn't find the information booklet telling me how to get to the Gym and for the life of me I could not find the air conditioning control, nor in fact the air conditioning unit. Despite all of these omissions the Plume of Feathers and its bunkhouse will remain in my memory for eternity as a most welcome oasis in a desert of fatigue.

5

Saturday 16th June 2007
Day 2

Up at 07:00, no time for breakfast. The plan was set: today we were going to try and get back on schedule. 88 miles to the Lizard then back 180 miles to the border with Wales and on 100 miles into Wales. 368 miles would get us back on track. We would then be able to relax for the next 7 days of riding.

Chris broke the news; he had to be back at home in Lewisham by Friday 22nd to pick up Maddie from school. This reduced our total available time from nine or ten days to six and a half, this meant our daily mileage count had just risen from 244 to 354 (given our disastrous first day). Chris suggested that we keep to the original pace and he would peel off and head home ahead of the journey ending.

The Ride

This was simply not an option, he was central to this journey there was no way the team was going to be split, and besides, it was now a real challenge.

Morning on the moor was damp, cold and unwelcoming. This truly was the Baskerville country that Sir Arthur Conan Doyle described so well. The mist lay like a sheet with the heather growing through it. Sheep ambled nonchalantly along the sides of the road, completely un-phased by the bikes and even the un-baffled overtures of my massive, testosterone charged 1340 V-Twin engine had no effect whatsoever, other than to draw a look of absolute disgust from the ewes overseeing their young, a look, which I must say made me feel very small and extremely guilty. I resolved to ride more quietly, something which is all but impossible on a Harley. As we rode the weather brightened up a little and the mist gave way to a brighter, warmer morning, though none of us had the confidence to shed our waterproofs.

The roads remained small and the weather held off, as a result the roads dried sufficiently for me to relax further in my riding. It was easier, more natural, for me to lift my head and follow the lines defined by Chris and Paul. Though I buried deep any temptation to take the lead or second place in the ride. With those guys in front I had my benchmark. Two experienced riders and Chris's Satellite Navigation system and I felt very safe.

I should be completely honest when describing my confidence in the Satellite Navigation system. At the outset, some 120 miles earlier both Paul and I had expressed great interest, even fascination at the space age technology that was to become referred to as the SatNav. So much so that we had suggested that Chris lead the first leg of the journey down through the West Country, despite the fact that we live in the West Country, and know it like the back of our own hands. Chris programmed the desired destination from Bleaden Village to The Lizard on the first day and the SatNav proceeded to take us, through the centre of Bridgewater, not the hottest tourist spot in Britain, off the bypass and into the centre of Taunton, a city locked tight in traffic from dawn till dusk, even on a Sunday, so Friday afternoon was just magical. Missed Tiverton completely and ended up on Motorway Junction 27 before we wrestled back control. We bypassed Exeter and headed out on the A30 then left at Moretonhampstead and into deepest Dartmoor. The problem with SatNav is that if you know an area you will always know better than the dulcet toned cyber chick (who if ever you have the option, sounds fantastic in Spanish). She is only ever of real use if you genuinely do not know where you are going or if you need to get out of an unfamiliar city quickly but need to end up on the right road. Beyond these applications she pervasively lures you into a false sense of security, robs you of your common sense and then sends you on a wild goose chase, and all the time you will be extolling her virtues to all of your friends. In truth this sexy young mistress has little substance and will never be a substitute for the one hundred percent reliable, easy to follow, route map. Partners on the road for more years than you can remember, always right and always giving you all of the information, trusting you to glean what is relevant and what is not. I always feel better being given a maximum of information and the time to make up my own mind. Miss SatNav tells you only what she thinks is relevant, this is rarely enough, but the ride is sometimes very exciting and always novel. The best option is probably to take a leaf out of Francois Mitterand's book, have SatNav installed but keep your reliable Map. Hopefully the two will not meet until, as in his case, at the funeral.

As we approached our first goal we passed Goonhilly down, this is a satellite earth station on the southern most tip of the UK mainland. A surreal place built in the days of Quatermass and American B Movies. The centre was, and I suspect still is, the core of voice and data communications for a large part of the Northern Hemisphere. I had the good fortune to visit the place ten years earlier with a colleague named Patrick. We were both working for a large corporation with me heading up the operation and Patrick at the head of all IT and Telecoms development for the business. We represented one of British Telecoms largest customers which led to some fascinating corporate entertainment. This particular visit I must confess was more fascinating for Patrick than for me, though I do have a lasting memory of the Goonhilly Down control centre. In those days it was an enormous room which resembled the bridge of the Starship Enterprise and was staffed entirely by people who would look completely at home at one of its conventions. One had some Spock ears on his computer another had far too many pictures of Diana Troy and one even wore a badge which read 'beam me up Scotty'. In the centre of the control room was a desk full of levers and buttons and in the centre of this was a huge red button, about three inches in diameter, emblazed across the front of it were the words 'DO NOT TOUCH'. This to Patrick was like a water slide on a sunny day or a bus lane in a traffic jam. He sidled over to the console and stared at the button, then cool as you like reached out and deftly pushed the button. At which point two of the Trekkies looked up and said, 'there's always one'... Patrick went on to develop and implement three of the largest IT/Telecoms programmes the UK has ever seen. Never restrained by dictate or instruction and with probably the best and most systemic mind of anyone I have ever encountered, he will always push the wrong buttons and get the right results. Except on this occasion, when the Geeks prevailed. I wonder how many times a week they got to laugh at that joke.

Though still dry the weather remained overcast threatening rain. The landscape now indicated a far different weather pattern to the one we were experiencing. Gardens were filled with amazing plants, every other house with a Palm Tree, some quite large, the foliage hinting at warm summers. The weather betraying a November chill. We rode through a square of shops and down a narrowing path until the road ran out and turned into a muddy track, this gave onto a small sloping car park with a tea house, souvenir shop and a spectacular view of a troubled ocean. Dark cliffs, rocky islands and an angry sky. It was 11:00 on the 16th June and we were standing on the Southerly most tip of the UK mainland, next to an old couple from Bodmin who came down once a week for a cup of tea and a slice of Carrot Cake. The sense of achievement was overwhelming.

The Liquorice Road

Photographs and documentary evidence duly gathered we headed back up the track and by 11:15 we were sitting in a café ordering a Full English without beans but with an extra order of mushrooms, toast and two cups of tea each. Chris, being a vegetarian munched his way through a slight variation of this culinary classic.

It was 12 noon and we wanted to cover 280 more miles before the end of the day. As we looked north the sky looked unwelcoming. The impression was clear: if we were going back up through the Peninsula it was going to be hard work. In addition we would be riding past Plymouth again, Plymouth, where there is a regular ferry to Santander in northern Spain, where it was 38°C, beer is served cold and fuel is cheaper. We decided that if we had any chance of staying on target we would need to use the Motorway between Exeter and Bristol. No sooner had we left The Lizard and the skies opened, this was a biblical downpour under which we remained for the next two hours, slowing our progress to a painful crawl. The scenery obliterated by spray and mist. The preceding two hours having yielded only 110 miles. The rains ceased as we pulled into a service station for a coffee, fuel and a team chat. My waterproofs had completely failed and it was becoming increasingly obvious that the way I had packed my bike was not helping me ride. I had loaded everything I had on the back of the bike, which made the front exceptionally light and "skippy", in the wet weather this was making cornering very difficult, it was apparent now that this had not helped me on the previous day when trying to get around the tight Dartmoor lanes. We agreed to head for Riders. This is a large motorcycle dealership in Bridgewater about sixty miles away. Here I could try and buy some better waterproofs and Paul could get some gloves which did not attract water. Chris was in heaven, his bike designed for adverse conditions; his kit repelled enough water to make dry-suit diving in the north-sea a viable option. At the outset I found it quite amusing how Chris could be so all-consumed by ensuring he had enough kit to cover every eventuality. I was now extremely envious. I vowed to listen and learn. We agreed to ride until 4pm, if at that point we were not past the Avon Bridge we would stop at home, dry off and re-group in the morning.

No sooner had we started riding and the skies opened again, this time worse than before, we were on the Motorway and travelling at 35 miles per hour, my MP3 player was set to random play. Talking Heads *'We're on a road to nowhere,'* started playing. I could feel the spirit of adventure exiting my body. We left the M5 at Bridgwater and Riders appeared in all its glory, under a pillar of brilliant sunlight which tore through the clouds to light our way.

Riders has a café where hardcore sunny weekend bikers in pristine Harley Davidson leathers flock to be seen. I didn't care, a coffee and then upstairs to the bargain bucket. Nothing in my size. Clever.

Bargain in Riders has a different meaning to anywhere else in the English speaking world. They have the West Country monopoly for the sale of Harley Davidson and as a result are able to charge pretty much what they like or at least that is the way it seems. In fairness on the lines that can be sold elsewhere they are pretty keen and the parts/accessories team and the service team are really helpful people. My own experience of the sales team however is poor and I have not encoun-

The Ride

tered anyone with the inclination to speak highly of them. They sell because Harleys sell and they are the only guys who sell them. Unfortunately this gives Harley a very poor reputation, shame because it's a great outlet and an awesome product. My plea to the Harley Davidson Motorcycle Company is a simple one, grant somebody else licence to sell your product in the West Country please! And show these guys the benefit of some competition. I've tried complaining twice, in writing. No response. I have since diverted my loyalties and affections to Morses Motorcycles in Weston, a family run business which should be regarded as an oasis in a desert of customer service ambivalence, always friendly, always expert advice. I found some overalls and some better gloves, Paul did the same. We paid and we headed on our way.

We decided to head straight for home and regroup at 07:30. We were not going to try for mid-Wales, we were tired and wet. Chris had ridden 150 miles more than Paul and I and we were already worn down by poor weather and in my case sub-standard kit. 360 miles in one and a half days was pretty disappointing but the thought of another four hours in the rain and then pitching a tent was even less welcoming and to be fair, probably a little foolish.

Paul pealed off one junction before us and headed home, we got to mine and strangely the skies were

clear. Chris immediately set to making some modi-
fications to his bike and I started to explore better
ways of packing and loading mine. I moved almost
a third of the load from the back of the bike to the
front handlebars. Chris rewired and fitted a new
power outlet but blew all the fuses. This would
have completely stressed me out and I would
probably have panicked and called an electrician,
not Chris. He traced the new wiring back to the
fault and fixed it, fitted a new fuse and we both put
the bikes in the garage.

My in-laws were staying and Emma needed to
spend time with them, time without me. They love
their daughter very much; I on the other hand,
whilst enjoying a good, though sometimes taught,
relationship, never truly met the standard a parent
requires for their daughter. This is fine and normal
for some…, I am not claiming to be a victim in this
relationship simply that at certain times, when they
have things to discuss, it is politic to stay away.

Chris and I went to my parents' place, they were
away for the summer in France so the peace and
tranquillity of an empty house was perfect. I cannot
remember what or if we ate, simply that a good
nights sleep followed. The only remark being that
we were far too tired to have only travelled 360
miles. With 1,840 miles to go in five and a half
days we would need some better weather. I believe

in no gods and therefore had no direction in which to honestly direct my prayers. I drifted off to sleep having looked at the BBC weather forecast for both the next 24 hours and the 5 day extended forecast and by trying to calculate the probability of us riding under each of the aggressive weather systems ravaging the UK mainland, before they actually broke.

I was quietly content that the rains could not get any worse and that so far all bikes and riders had performed well.

Sunday 17th June 2007
Day 3
(1,840 to go)

A mixture of bright skies and dark clouds, but we are feeling pretty positive. I brewed a pot of coffee and we get ourselves sorted, birds are even singing in the trees. I thank our lord of infinite improbability for the delivery of what could possibly be a dry start to the day. The fact that I have now invested in a decent set of waterproofs the strongest indicator of dry weather ahead.

The Ride

Paul arrives at 07:30 and we head straight for Wales, over the new bridge and towards the Celtic Manor, then due north past Monmouth on clear, open roads with long bends, none too tight. The skies stayed clear all morning and the riding was blissful. We reluctantly stopped for breakfast and fuel after 120 miles, 120 miles in only 2 hours! This was fantastic; our lord of the blessed improbability had granted us a clear morning, each stretch of road just waiting to be ridden, not fast or slowly, just ridden.

Breakfast consisted of a cup of strong coffee and a Bacon Sandwich. Our arrival at the diner corresponded with what appeared to be the weekly breakfast of the Mid-Wales chapter of the 'not quite a fully fledged' back patch bikers gang. It did include a few, hardcore looking bikers, the statutory fat trike rider guy holding court, and the two or three slightly Gothic looking women who should have discarded the leather about ten years earlier (or bought bigger looser versions). As we entered they deployed the well rehearsed, silent, slightly bored with all other biker's routine. Their performance shattered of course by us smiling and saying "hello". Their entire routine and persona was of course designed to ward off the 'happy communicator' their presence designed to instil fear and loathing. Obviously we followed up our greeting with a long smile and by maintaining eye contact.

Faced with such an impenetrable challenge they quickly caved in a replied. "Hello, looks like we are going to have a lovely day for a ride out", "are you going far, you look pretty loaded up?" We gave them all of the information and they retreated wounded to their coven to lick their wounds.

Actually that is not all together fair, I have not yet met a group of bikers who were not friendly and helpful to all they encountered, even and possibly more so the organised Side and Back Patch gangs. I have never known them start trouble and never known any of them wantonly perpetuate it. Two groups in particular with whom I have had good experiences are the Van Diemans and the Outriders, all of whom appear to be honourable people. Of course one gentleman sporting a Predators Back Patch and riding an FXD once spat on my car whilst queuing for the Dartford Tunnel. I still have his number.

The Ride

After breakfast we rode on, but not before we had
shed the waterproofs. The roads continued to be
quick, clear and fantastic fun. Riding head up,
sweeping into and out of the bends, over the ridges
and undulations, the bike hugging the corners, accelerating out of each onto the straight before
easing back in preparation for catapulting out of the
next. These roads carried us all the way to Chesterfield and to our next fuel stop. We had not seen
much of Wales which was a great shame, but the
roads were impeccable, the American Diner was
"luvlee and fablas", it was 12:30 and we had already completed 240 miles. Throughout these four
hours of riding my MP3 player had randomly se-
lected perfect tracks, ranging from *The Who*

The Liquorice Road

through *John Martyn* to *The Stranglers* and *St Germain*, and of course everything in between.

We decided that if we could get past the major cities of Chester and Liverpool quickly we would have time to cut across at Kendal and head for Lake Windermere. This was 95 miles away but the roads were big, the weather was holding and we had friends waiting, who some years earlier had left London and the corporate existence for what we would all say was a more sensible way of life. Whether it actually was, only they could say.

I had met Paul and Eva twice about 16 years earlier in the South West of France from where we all travelled over the border into Spain for the Fiesta de San Fermin. These trips were subsequent to the initial trip made with Chris in 1989. Like Chris, both Paul and Eva were journalists; hence they stayed in close contact. Welcomed with open arms, the intrusion of our noisy bikes did little to rattle what was a most idyllic settling. Paul and Eva had used the intervening time between our meetings to create three delightful daughters. The welcome of their beaming faces huge smiles and a cold beer was better than perfect after the long days ride. Tall House is, I believe, Edwardian, with an altogether individual configuration, all of which culminated in a room at the top offering a panoramic view of the Cumbrian Mountains. From the garden terrace all we could do was stand in silence watching the mist and cloud rolling over the peaks which stood before us. Shards of radiant warm sunlight with mirror-bright silver linings appeared and faded, as if smothered by heavy dark shrouds. I suggested setting a camera up on a tripod and taking exactly the same photograph at the same time every day for a year, prepared to guarantee that they would get 365 completely different photographs. Eva pointed out that she could look out of the window every five minutes and it would never be the same. If I worked from this environment I should never get a thing done.

I was honoured as the children grabbed me by the hand and insisted on giving me a tour of the gar-

The Liquorice Road

den. These fascinating children were genuinely interested in their world as though imbued with the spirit of the Lost Boys they seemed even more interested in showing this world to me. This was followed by each of the girls insisting on playing us tunes on their various instruments, all completely unprompted by the parents. Thinking back to my own Danielle and Jo, Chris' Ben and Maddie and Paul's boy Ryan, I couldn't help thinking how staggeringly lucky we all were, so far we were all parents of similarly fascinating children, articulate, polite, interesting, interested and above all respectful. So far my experience of the youth of Mainland Britain bore little resemblance to that which our press so frequently portrayed.

The children evaporated into the background as the meal commenced. Fine food, great wine, 5 bottles of great wine, and some increasingly lively banter, all made up a fantastic evening; one of those evenings which we all wish wouldn't end so quickly. The conversations ranged from the wonders of dangerous drivers on the A36 to Richard Dawkins' systematic dismantling of Christianity via every other conceivable subject, all liberally smattered with a huge amount of laughter and plenty of ribbing. No conclusions were reached.

The Ride

We retired to our beds having ridden 325 great miles, caught up a little on our target, restored our confidence in the challenge and spent a fantastic evening with friends. We were all asleep before heads hit pillows.

Monday 18th June
Day 4
(1,514 to go)

Semi early start, we will all claim this was due to the gallant self sacrifice we made in order not to disturb this family's morning ritual. Which was as finely tuned as every other modern family tribal ritual? The truth was that we all had hangovers from our share of the five bottles of Claret. A perfectly behaved Eleanor brought us each a reviving cup of tea. 07:15 we headed for our bikes.

The Ride

Chris' bike fired up first time like a faithful Labrador ready to spring to his master's side as and when called. My *Wide Glide* reluctantly grunted a few times as if being woken from a deep sleep and then roared at me like an angry lion, insisting his kingdom wake with him. Chris and I screamed up the drive and out onto the highway for another day of riding. Paul's bike clicked, then clicked again, and then clicked. Chris and I waited patiently at the top of the hill, as patiently as any child waiting to go on a great adventure. Neither keen to turn back, even the 50 metres. After a few minutes we silently gave in and turned back, only to find Paul bravely pushing the GPZ up the gravel path, by the time we got to him he didn't need our help. A feather of guilt floated by on the morning breeze. "It's my starter I think" he called through his visor as he rolled the bike down hill and jumped on. Sure enough she sparked up and purred like a contented kitten, afforded the spoilt attention she craved.

We had agreed to follow Chris on a route he and Paul had worked out for us; this was not going to be a fast morning's riding. We were heading for the heart of the Cumbrian Mountains. Tight winding roads, steep inclines, poor road surfaces and sheep. Everything the *Wide Glide* hates and everything the Africa Twin loves. Paul on the GPZ with is experience and the bikes agility was indifferent, I don't think there was anything the two of them would be concerned about. I resolved to hang back and take things at my speed. Rushing, and forcing the pace, I was quickly learning, leads to some really boring, stressful and often quite dangerous riding, not least because the *Wide Glide* weighs in excess of 270kgs + payload compared with the more agile 200kgs of the other bikes. I guess anyone planning to cross a mountain range in an armchair should be content to take it at a relaxed pace.

People had spoken to me of how striking the Cumbrian Mountains were, though nothing had prepared me for quite how staggeringly beautiful this region was. As we wound our way up the patchwork roads, littered with potholes, and signs warning of the dangers of taking any vehicle, other than a packhorse over the Hardknott Pass, we were greeted with scenes as spectacular as anything born of Tolkien's imagination. The occasional Landrover came the other way; each looked and sounded unlikely to reach its destination, all carrying a beaming weathered face one rolled up sleeve and a forearm the size of Popeye's.

Passing over the top of the Pass, the road ahead tumbled down the centre of a most spectacular, green valley, so large and broad that it commanded the entire view. Cleft by a winding road which meandered its way like a stream entering its twilight years to what seemed like infinity. Nothing approached, and there was nothing on the path to hinder progress. This vision did not possess me with the desire to go fast as you might imagine, more the desire to find a pace that suited both the *Wide Glide* and me and to savour the moment, like keeping the best morsel for the last mouthful.

Two hours to cover 25 miles, but what a rewarding quarter century. My riding had improved no end, and strangely, my focus on the problems I brought away with me to solve. I had stopped looking down at the road and was looking up, up towards the horizon, I was rediscovering my vision. This sounds corny but the clarity was frightening. Riding toward a horizon meant the corners and bends I encountered became fun, pleasant, actually really enjoyable. In the past each corner was a challenge, a chore, a risk. Now I was gliding through them and powering towards my goal. I had never enjoyed riding like this. How could I lift my head and find my horizon, how could I find that goal. The journey was becoming so enjoyable that for the first time in my life I was enjoying the act of 'doing' as much as the prospect of achievement. I had in my youth been a pretty successful athlete (not an international but pretty good), I won many prizes for 100m and 400m, I hated running but loved winning. I had a successful corporate career. I hated and despised the act of working but loved the recognition of all in the hierarchy. And so the tale of woe rolled on. Now for the first time I was enjoying the journey, my own company, the knowledge that three of us were working together, and the challenge of achievement. I hadn't a care for any acknowledgement or recognition. Reaching the four compass points of the UK mainland had become the unavoidable goal that made the journey possible. It existed only to facilitate the journey. I declared to make this my mission moving forward and dedicate my thoughts to finding a goal in life which would facilitate my journey. I undertook to start enjoying life's journey.

The Ride

Just over the mountains and time to stop for break-fast. The village of Gosforth appeared like a mercurial sunrise promising joy and sustenance in the form of 'Full *English*' accompanied by a cup of tea. For all of the culinary misrepresentation, England actually possesses, when well prepared with quality produce, the most gastronomic breakfast on the planet. The balance of flavours you get from fresh eggs, bacon, Cumberland sausages, mushrooms, grilled tomatoes, fried bread and black pudding is blissful. Each mouthful reminding the devourer of what a great empire it is that finds its centre on this sceptred isle.

The meal was ably served with characteristic charm and humour by an Irish girl called Karen and cooked by a kind faced cook called Rushka from Poland. Some would see this as a dilution of the great nation I speak so proudly of, but not me. The concept of open borders and the welcome, free movement of hard working people are, I believe, healthy for both the Gene Pool and our broader culture. The fact that people strive so hard to come to this land, and then work so hard to master its core cultural icons, such as the *'Full English'* is further proof that we are getting it right. I am of course working on a strategy for encouraging the mass exodus of some of our home grown prodigy to places which could use a massive investment of hard, directed labour. Their initiation into the ways of other cultures and a little hard work might serve to transform their loathing, which is born of fear, into welcoming respect.

Replete, we set ourselves the days challenge, Scotland! By breaking a few rules we could get onto the Motorway at Carlisle and head straight for Glasgow. This was going to be a long, boring ride but the promise of the A82 north of Glasgow was too much to resist.

As we rode the last of the winding roads through the villages south of Carlisle I noted many a proud, pristine doorstep. Well swept, painted, with many supporting a small pot in full bloom. Sweeping bends and hard corners leading into the next row of terraces on parade, with their shiny doors, polished windows and beautifully dressed window boxes. A cider farm, a sign made from the cut out silhouettes of ducks and squat grey houses standing alone in fields like tombstones.

We quickly came back down to earth and then deep into what seemed like hell, in the form of the M6, M74 and the M8. We covered a lot of miles very quickly to get us past Glasgow. To our shame we missed all that this far northern part of England and Southern Scotland had to offer. We were lured off the Motorway once to pull into the service station for fuel and coffee. Primo Coffee and Jacket Potatoes! "We are Passionate about Coffee" the sign read. Perfect, we parked the bikes and headed for the coffee stand.

"Two Americanos and a Cappuccino please"
"We don't do those" came the reply
"Oh, OK three filter coffees please"
"I'll have to put on a new pot, would you like instant"?
"No, I thought you were Passionate about Coffee"?
"What"?
"Don't worry, I'll have three bottles of mineral water and three Jacket Potatoes please, two with Chilli and Cheese and one just with Cheese please".

The Liquorice Road

"We haven't got any Jackets; they will take about half an hour"
"I thought you sold Jacket Potatoes"
"We do, but we had a very busy lunch time, people don't usually ask for them in the afternoon"
"But its only 1 o'clock, isn't that lunchtime?"
"What?"
"Just three bottles of water please"
"£3.90 please, would you like anything else with that?"
"Yes please, two Americano's, one Cappuccino and three Jacket Potatoes"
"What?"
"No thanks that's fine"
Fantastic, Primo Coffee, Passionate about customer Service....

The problem was that Wales and the Cumbrian Mountains had spoiled us for good riding and the lure of the roads across the West Highlands was too much to resist. We pressed on.

Our souls were obviously too pure and we were quickly ejected from the hell of Motorway travel onto the paradise that was the A82 north of Glasgow. The roads were immediately improved; they became progressively clearer, the surfaces better and the scenery, almost immediately breathtaking. We skirted Loch Long and headed up towards Loch Lomond, the bends skimming the water or running close into the cliff wall. The roads wide and smooth enough to hinder no progress, passing cars on this road was an absolute pleasure. Chris refusing to let even trucks get in his way. Like the Pigeon in the Wacky Races, nothing was going to stop Chris. He shot past an enormous truck carrying what appeared to be entire trees, this hindered Paul for a while and me for what seemed an age.

We stopped for coffee at the head of Loch Lomond. The filling station seemed to be in the middle of nowhere, though the queue for the toilet was longer than just the three of us. Whilst at Paul and Eva's house I had finally looked up the correct tire pressures for the *Wide Glide*. I seized the moment, which of course brought me a severe and

The Liquorice Road

justified telling off from my compatriots for not having attended to this detail at the outset of the journey. It was pointed out that the early poor handling due to negligent packing was probably compounded by a lack of the relevant pounds per square inch. I gathered my humility, agreed sheepishly and got on with the task in hand. We then sat quietly enjoyed our teas and coffees and said very little. One would have expected great torrents of conversation each time we dismounted but speech only tended to happen when required and as the journey progressed this became more, not less the case. This was not because people were not getting along, the opposite; we were getting to know each other so well that the surplus 70% of conversation which seems to dominate so much of our time was simply not required.

Fuelled and ready we continued on the A82 towards Fort William but resolved to turn left and take the ferry across Loch Linnch. The aim was to get as close as possible to Ardenamurchan Point by the end of the day.

Since passing Glasgow the weather had been fantastic and seemed to be getting better. The landscape exploded in front of us, revealing long open stretches of Tarmac, the roads beckoned like sultry temptresses, daring you to try them, daring you to just twist that grip and fly. The lure was too much; almost simultaneously we all hit the throttle and took off. I was so glad that a speed camera would have been considered blight on the landscape. After one particularly long run the road wound up a winding incline to a viewing point, giving a broad vista over the entire valley through which we had just ridden. It was occupied by a Hawker and lots of bikers. All had ridden the same valley and then seized the opportunity to stop and stare, in awe, at something which, if designed, must have been planned and drafted by a keen motorcyclist. This is the closest I will ever get to creationist belief, as I find it much more plausible that the laws of improbability conspired to generate this landscape and lay upon it a road of such high quality.

The Liquorice Road

I spotted a newspaper headline which reported the death of Bernard Manning, which was no laughing matter; mind you neither were his jokes.

We reached the ferry and waited a welcome 20 minutes, passing the time sitting in the sunshine enthusing about the roads we had just ridden. We were joined by the usual pedestrian enthusiast. He'd owned every kind of bike imaginable, rebuilt them all and ridden every biking pilgrimage on the planet. He just wanted to chat. We didn't mind, he did all of the talking and we provided the timely nods. He soon got himself onto the subject of his business. It transpires that he and his wife had sold up house, home, wagon and horses and bought a B&B on the Isle of Mull, basing their business model on 85-100% occupancy they set about building a new life, they were getting about 30% occupancy and struggling to sell the business before going under. This was a sobering message to those of us easily drawn into the endless stream of lifestyle TV which constantly extols the virtues of changing our approach, to everything. He then, somehow, got onto the subject of his dental hygiene problems and pending medical interventions. The ferry gates opened and we bolted, in such a hurry to board, we nearly forgot the bikes.

Arriving on the other side it was clear that we were slowing down. The well positioned pub ensured that no more progress would be made for another hour. All enjoyed a pint of Heavy and discussed our next move. We were about 50 miles from Ardnamurchan, and tired. This said we were keen to get as close as possible. After some time we decided to push on. Chris set off first with his trusty Sat Nav leading the way, the choice was East or West, otherwise referred to as the Wrong way or the Right way. The Sat Nav went East, Paul and I went West, Chris caught up and re-took the lead. The roads quickly narrowed to tight single lane tracks and whilst the surfaces were good the narrow winding roads were, in places, quite hard work. This said they were very rewarding and not the threat they would have been had we encountered them on the first day. I still lacked the confidence to follow at the speed that Chris and Paul travelled but skilfully avoided feeling guilty every time they were forced to stop and wait for me.

We reached Salen 22 miles shy of our goal at about 7pm and decided to stop at the Salen Hotel. This beautiful little hotel and restaurant seemed to all intent a purpose to be perfect. A nice bar and an excellent menu promised a good evening. And so it was, we drank well, ate handsomely and then proceeded to feed the midges, every last drop of blood in our bodies. For anyone who has never experienced this plague, it is relentless. They are almost

The Ride

invisible, accept when they gather in groups of a million or more, which they do constantly all around the West Highlands, all around Salen, all around me. The landlord joyfully explained that they are attracted to exhaled air and that it is only the females that bite. I tried to stop breathing; I seriously considered not breathing until we got out of Scotland and as for the question of gender identification, who was ever going to test his theory/assertion? The sad truth of this was that the couple who owned this place were obviously pouring heart and soul into what was a really fantastic place. The experience they had designed and implemented was just lovely and the meal excellent, but they were always going to be at war with this discriminate swarm, hell bent on driving away their customers. I hope somehow that the swarm fails and the females at least are banished, causing the species to die out within the next 12 months.

I left the boys in the bar after dinner and retired to my room.

Tuesday 19th June 2007
Day 5
(1,224 to go)

Ardnamurchan was only 22 miles away but it had been pouring with rain all night and the roads were set to get smaller and even more winding. The landlord of the Salen Hotel was adamant that the journey would take no more than 40 minutes each way. So we set off at 07:30, aiming to be back at 09:30 for breakfast.

The bikes were parked right outside of our rooms for a quick getaway; this said we still got eaten alive just getting onto our bikes. I actually put all of my leathers on in my room and went outside with my crash helmet on. I made the fatal mistake of leaving my visor up, as a result the entire West

The Ride

Highlands population of female midges decided to have a drinks morning in my helmet, guess what drink was on the menu.

The roads were wet and quite slippery, this compounded by the fact that much of this road had recently been resurfaced thanks to a European Development Grant. Wet, gravely and very slippery, it got worse, very occasionally an oncoming driver who was not used to meeting traffic coming the other way; as a result he/she would be travelling at quite a speed, causing both the lead rider and car to lunge into an emergency stop. The track wound around the shoreline revealing the most beautiful sheltered bays and inlets, the water dark and still like a mirror; on closer inspection it was crystal clear.

There were signs of life everywhere, fishing boats, cars on driveways, even little houses but apart from the occasional oncoming car, there was nobody. It was as if all the people had been removed from the landscape. As we left the last signs of human life behind and turned up onto the hills the vista was astounding. We skirted the side of a steep hill, looking down and across a huge valley to the right. Watching the road trail away in front of us, the next mile and a half painted onto the landscape ahead. The road now was pretty poor, craggy and full of potholes. Chris powered ahead on the Africa Twin

forward and down the track before us. As he and
Paul disappeared over the end of this great valley
they startled a young stag and his harem. He appeared on top of a hillock standing proud with his 8
to 10 points and girls all around him. Momentarily
still, he stood silhouetted against a troubled High-
land sky, and then coolly trotted out of sight. I felt
honoured and elated to see him, guilty for having
disturbed his peaceful morning.

We rode on over the moorland with heather clad
hills, the deep green and rich dark purple vegeta-
tion dotted at dabbed by the occasional sheep,
looking on in disgust. The sky a mish mash of angry cloud and brilliant white streams of sunshine
breaking through to light the way, as though some
celestial presence was pointing out the location of a
great treasure, it was, Western Scotland!

Crossing a stone bridge and we came upon a single
track, walled road with a traffic light controlling
access. A thirty second wait and we were permitted
to venture forward, the stretch of road wound
around the headland to reveal a small grey stone
single story building, a slight rise and another more
industrial construction. The view, whilst stunningly
beautiful, was subdued, it felt as though it was
shrouded in a veil of silence, but for some unknown reason it felt to me as though it just wanted
to scream. This did not strike me as a peaceful

The Ride

place. Whether it was the anticipation of getting there or the sheer beauty of the short journey we had just travelled I do not know, but the place felt troubled. This could well be an unjustified comment, but it didn't feel like a happy place. If it were my child I would have carefully chosen the moment to ask "is there anything you want to tell me"?

The three of us stood in silence and looked at the dank, misty, sun pierced view. A few pictures were taken, Chris commented on how slowly I was riding and we started to prepare for or return to Salen. Chris woke the keeper of the grey stone building in order to buy a sticker for his panniers. We waited dutifully at the lights and then headed away back over the moors, hoping, longing to see the young stag again.

No such luck, he and his harem were long gone, or hiding well behind the hillocks and crags.

Panic struck both Paul and me. We had completely forgotten to fill up with fuel and were running dangerously low. There had been a point as we turned off of the beautifully re-groomed, European-funded road, where we had seen a hand painted sign claiming that fuel was available a few miles in the wrong direction. We started the search, that panicked, ill-informed kind of search where you find yourself feeling sick at your own stupidity. The nagging question; cut and run for a main road or follow the signs, the hand written signs, un-branded, uninformative, tantalisingly dangerous signs. Eventually we came upon a shop and on the other side of the road a disused petrol pump. We went in to ask. This was it; this was the fossil fuel oasis at the end of our quest. I politely asked the girl at the counter, who was visibly shocked by my presence, if we could purchase some fuel, she nodded in my general direction and then nervously called out a name. I am assuming it was a name, in fact it was a sound that I had never heard before and not one I am about to venture to spell. A few painfully long seconds later Martina Navratilova came out from the rear of the shop and looked straight at me,

The Ride

without missing a step she spoke, "Petrol or Diesel?" I was so intimidated that I momentarily forgot. "Well?" uh, petrol, unleaded. I drew breath, pulled myself together and realised that I had just been intimidated for the first time in about 20 years, by a tennis star lookalike. Having come to my senses I focused on the knackered old petrol pump that was wailing at my bike as its eyes spun around and around. I had not seen one of these pumps in action since my distant youth. Slowly my eyes tuned into another hand written sign propped up against the side of the pump, my mouth started to work before my brain. "£1.08 per litre, are you planning on retiring in the next few weeks?" clearly I was no longer feeling intimidated, well it had been a long time since she competed seriously. She coldly raised her eyes from the pump and with the closest to a smile I think she had pulled all morning simply said, "where else are y'going to go?" I resolved to feel intimidated again. I even bought one of their 'wicked home made brownies' as I paid over my hard earned cash. Next time I am required to put together a really 'hard arsed' team for a job; I'm coming to get Martina.

The bikes replete we headed back towards the Hotel for breakfast. Riding along the coast path I glanced down towards a beach lying below the road. A beautiful half mooned inlet with a narrow band of sand and a perfectly groomed strip of lush green lawn following its contour as if stitched onto the hem of a pretty dress. Trotting along the water line, alone and unhurried was another young stag. It seemed so perfectly at home but completely out of place. I had never seen nor dreamed of such an image. I stopped and cut the engine. Just staring at the graceful, self assured independence with which he was patrolling the border between land and sea. I was elated, I knew that I would never see this again, which didn't sadden me, I don't think I ever want to experience that particular moment again, it was too good, too special, like feeling the grip of my daughter's newborn hand, or the midwife directing me to loosen my shirt in order that she could place my newborn son inside it to warm him up. Moments too precious to repeat, moments which drilled deep into the consciousness as if to plant the seed of a perfect memory that would grow and flower so as to move me whenever recalled.

The Ride

Riding away from this was heart wrenching but I had to press on, not least because Chris was getting more than a little miffed at my slow progress. The weather started to degenerate into a misty, penetrating rain. I thanked the lord of infinite improbability again for having held off the deluge until now. I caught up with the boys just as we re-entered Salen, two elderly gentlemen chatted by the roadside, one with a fishing rod in hand, obviously on his way out and one with a shotgun and a rabbit, on his way home, the pace here was different. We pulled into the hotel some considerable time after we had planned, the Landlord quickly pointing out that the time for breakfast had long passed. The chef took pity, knocked up a feast, and earned a place in our history.

The Liquorice Road

Breakfast finished, we set ourselves a ridiculous goal; this was a goal which would not only put us on schedule but ahead of it. We had already been riding since 07:30, despite this and buoyed by our replete stomachs we decided that Dunnet Head, the most Northerly tip of the UK mainland, was achievable. We elected to leave our waterproofs off and set off on what we knew was going to be a mammoth day.

The roads were perfect, clear and impeccably tuned to each rider's abilities and as unlikely as that might sound each rider rode with a style and confidence like never before on this journey. Each corner just cried out to be ridden faster and harder than the last. Cars and trucks were no obstacle. If the bikes could have flown they would have. When we finally stopped for a coffee the exuberance whilst clear was all but silent, I think "Wow" and "Jeeeesus" were the only vaguely meaningful words uttered. The 861, 830 and A82 had delivered some awesome riding, a combination of clear weather, exquisite roads and what could now, finally, be described as synergy between man and beast (bike). For 30 minutes communications were restricted to smiles and strange noises all meant to purvey the same message, that the last hour and a half had been spectacular. The Little Chef provided coffee and burgers, fuel next door and hard on to

The Ride

Inverness. The riding slowed somewhat as the tourist traffic thickened. This was not enough to dampen the spirits, progress was still strong and Inverness was upon us in no time. One more fill up before heading out towards the A9. I was accosted by another pedestrian enthusiast. The usual one way conversation, he'd owned them all, raced some of them and rebuilt half of them, he bimbled off but not before telling me about any impending interventions or debilitating illnesses. My rehearsed "piss off I'm bored now" look was obviously not working as well as it should have.

The rain stayed away but as we crossed the Moray Firth the wind picked up and started to buffet and pummel the bike. I shrank back into my seat and literally rode out the storm. Al Stewart, '*Stormy Monday Blues*' came over the MP3 player followed by '*Why does it always rain on me.*' What was driving the MP3 player? I banged the skip button a few times and found The Ruts, '*Babylon is Burning*'', hit the throttle and cleared the causeway at 120, which on a Harley in a strong wind is a bit like trying to write a letter whilst riding a Roller Coaster. Once over the causeway the wind backed off and things became a little more civilised. Despite my speedy crossing Chris and Paul were nowhere to be seen. We pushed on until Helmsdale, where little stirred until three well weathered men rolled out of the pub, stumbling as if it were

The Liquorice Road

3am, it was only 3pm. We entered the pub just in time for me to get a call from work. A distressed client, a foolish error followed by junior staff member attempting a cover up, they were about to get found out and needed me to get them out of trouble. A brief conversation made it clear that I was not going to cover anything up and some decisive guidance was issued. For once they listened and went public with the cock up and managed their way out of it. This conversation was to occupy my mind for the next few miles, though not as many as you might imagine.

Heading out of Helmsdale we dispensed with the A9, electing to head due north over Sutherland. Having first topped up our tanks, we had been told that the road over Sutherland was extremely remote with no services whatsoever, caution was exercised. The filling station in Helmsdale was staffed by a young overweight teenager wearing tracksuit bottoms and a Rangers football shirt, sitting in the back of the office were two more equally sizeable girls, all three should have been in school though the lad was obviously in charge of the place. He said little, but the larger of his two assistants exercised a remarkably confident questioning technique, especially as she freely launched her enquiries at people she didn't know.

"Where ya from"

The Ride

"Have ya been ti y'America"
"Wotsit laike"
"Is it laike Miami Vice"?
Answer *"No"*
The questions stopped.

The road out of Helmsdale quickly reduced to a single track, fairly straight, undulating gently, every two hundred metres a bulbous widening of the track to allow passing vehicles. On the western side of the track was a river which clearly offered great prizes. We passed several well booted Range Rovers and Pathfinders equipped with fishing rod holders on the bonnet. These rested majestically on the banks whilst their drivers stood waist deep in the rapids waving rod and line back and forth, the sun, electrifying the lines momentarily as they snaked through the air. I had once tried fly fishing, having signed up for a casting lesson at Blagdon Lake in Somerset. It was fascinating, bloody difficult, I used muscles I didn't know I had and still failed dismally. A stark reminder that there are no short cuts in life, not even for leisure activities. I didn't stick with it, like many things. I should have.

The Liquorice Road

The road became more and more remote, seem-
ingly unending and, at first pretty uninteresting.
The vista was opening up into a huge, wide, spectacular shallow valley. Not at all lush or green,
reminiscent of the hard planes of the Rockies
where rugged cattle and sheep eke out a living
munching on the least nutritious of all plant life.
There was nothing else on this road, the river
peeled away from us leaving a solitary straight,
single track which gently slopped away from us
and diminished in its distant perspective. The gentle winding undulation lulling us away to another
place, a place where fatigue evaporated and we
simply glided silently across the landscape. Despite
riding one of the loudest motorcycles in the world I
was possessed of an incredible, deep serenity. The

music had stopped some miles earlier and I was at peace. The sound of the bike had become white noise, as comforting as the sound of the womb.

For the first time in about ten years, more, for the first time ever, I knew everything I needed. Where my priorities were and what I had to do. This was not a bright lights moment, no great epiphany; the choirs of angels had not come to this show. It was me, my bike, my friends up ahead and an enormous smile on my face. I had simply realised how easy everything could and should be.

The bike pulled me over a little hillock as the track gently turned right. At its peak we were presented with a most beautiful view, the moors had become lush and green, with rich purple heathers and white speckles of flowers everywhere. Sheep dabbed the landscape and deer bolted over the far horizon. The craggy surface we had been riding for the last hour was replaced by a brand new, jet black roll of Liquorice that had been lovingly wound across this Daliesque landscape. It was perfect, so perfect it felt sacrilegious to ride it. A spotless road and a spotless moment. I never want to go back.

My time in this place was not spent planning what I was going to do or ruminating on what I had decided, there was no point, it was clear, unquestionable and simply too obvious to ponder further.

We broke out of the top of Sutherland onto the North Coast of Scotland and the temperature immediately went south, as far as we had gone north. We were riding, at speed along a freezing cold, windswept, bleak, grey, hellishly never ending road. There was no colour just shades of grey, even the police car which insisted on following us for 10 miles before doing a U-Turn, was grey. Thurso came and went, finally we turned left onto another single track, the deep green grass covered dunes were ravaged by a relentless wind, and this place was beautifully unwelcoming. We arrived at Dunnet Head just in time to see the sun bowing out of this incredible day, the colours were turned off and everything returned through dark blue to a deep cold black. The wind cutting across the Northern waters as though laden with razors. Scotland really has some harsh cold places, stunning, spectacular, wild and very tough.

For some insane reason we decided to see how far back down the A9 we could get before the fatigue beat us. A real and genuine fear set in, if we could not find civilisation before the exhaustion set in, we faced the clear and present danger of having to camp. Until now we had avoided this, much to Chris' chagrin, but now there was a genuine possibility that the campfire would have to be ceremonially lit. Paul and I exchanged a few worried glances. I then tore into my panniers and extracted two thick shirts and a substantial woollen hoody. Having put all of these on I then struggled to zip myself back into my leather jacket, I didn't care, I was going to be warm.

There was nothing pleasurable about the next 50 miles though the roads were good and empty. We were simply too tired to enjoy the ride. Like the stretch in Devon, forced to ride through the deluge, this too was a hard graft, the only difference being the lack of rain and the presence of extreme fatigue.

The villages passed without a second look, only slowing to inspect B&B signs, each hung with the mandatory 'No Vacancies' banner. We rode hard until we had gone full circle and we pulled into Helmsdale. The pub had no vacancies, but knew a Lady who had rooms, and promised to call her on our behalf. The warning was stark, "*it's late and she likes a drop, so don't be surprised if she's three sheets to the wind*". We didn't care.

As we turned right into the old court yard Chris decided to overtake me, this was possibly the most frightening moment in my 28 year motorcycling history. There was less than a Gnats testicle between his Africa Twin, my *Wide Glide* and both of our lives. The surge of Adrenaline brought with it several words starting with F and ending in a multitude of descriptive. Chris the hardened Dispatch Rider didn't register the issue, we were talking, and therefore we were not injured, what was the problem? There was logic to this response.

The old grey stone farm house was stunning, ragged and a bit tattered but absolutely stunning. Margery was a little on the happy side, but not so much that she could not make us welcome, she showed us to our respective rooms. The house had several reception rooms feeding away from a broad central hallway, this in turn gave to a wide arch launching the stairs. The place needed a few quid spending on it, but only a few. In fairness this was a beautiful happy house, obviously full of warm memories and Margery seemed fun, if a little squiffy.

The Liquorice Road

On the recommendation of our new friend we headed for a little restaurant in town. The place was full, which is generally a good sign. An electronic Hoola Dancer welcomed us in and ushered us past a bust of Elvis, the walls were festooned with photos of a gentleman in ladies clothes at various public events, each time attached to a frightened celebrity or dignitary. The venue was an exercise in *'extravagant'* décor. We had clearly found the home of one of the rarer members of this community and an environment which would have challenged less worldly guests, but in fairness this was a very welcome staging point. The less than inspiring menu more than compensated for by high cabaret and welcome smile.

What a day, after a late start to the journey we had now completed three of the four compass points, seen parts of our country that amazed us and found one of the most colourful restaurants in Scotland. These alone were memories that would buoy us through the next stage. Celebrations gave way to the downing of a final pint and a rapid retreat to our beds, beds which were not under canvas, another great achievement.

The Ride

This day alone had yielded three hundred and fifty two miles much of which was on single track roads - some of which was on the purest Liquorice, and some in what felt like blissful flight.

Wednesday 20th June 2007
Day 6
(872 to go)

A bright beaming smile and a well rehearsed question.

"Would'ya like Porridge or a Full Scottish Break-fast"?
"Yes" we replied.
"Both it is then".

The Ride

Margery you are a goddess, the breakfast put Helmsdale firmly onto our culinary map.

The plans and objectives were set out over breakfast, so tired by the previous day's riding the initial target was set at what we all quietly believed was too easily achievable. This said neither of us wanted to declare this belief public, in case the others resorted to violence. We were heading for Edinburgh. The breakfast was set to weigh heavily, but it was absolutely awesome and perversely, worth the pain. Fortunately we were not walking. As we packed up our bikes the weather started to close in on us. Since Devon we had been very fortunate, managing to avoid the majority of downpours. This sky looked both angry and unforgiving. Despite this we had come to believe in our invincibility. With echoes of a King Canute mentality we set off with our waterproofs stowed safely in our bags, that is all of us except Chris. As we rolled down the A9 towards Inverness we retraced our tracks for the second time on this journey. The wind and rain from the North Sea gnawingly cold, the coastline harsh and wind scarred, people hunched, with shoulders raised and heads buried low as though to shield them from this constant onslaught. Coming from the South West the prevailing wind is warm as it drives off of the Gulf Stream, welcoming and offering some familiarity and protection, this was different, this was a venge-

The Liquorice Road

ful cold and spiteful wind that would forgive no
oversight and exploit every opportunity to punish
your failure to prepare.

Despite this abrasive wind the weather held off
until just before Inverness. Having passed numer-
ous overhead signs offering severe weather
warnings we pushed on over the Moray Firth, Chris
dropped a gear and sped ahead and overtook a line
of cars whilst an 18 wheeler bore down on him.
Whilst still on the bridge we could see him disap-
pearing over the brow of the hill about a mile and a
half ahead. The skies tore open and the first sheet
of rain hit me as though Coco the Clown had
thrown a full bucket of water at me from about
three feet away. Paul and I pulled over and kitted
up in record time, then and continued riding, by
now we had no idea where Chris was. No matter
Edinburgh was the agreed destination. Visibility
was poor, the roads were busy and there was no
sign of a let up in the weather. Once passed Inverness we were riding an inland route and the wind
subsided, but not the rain. Varying between mist
and torrents it never stopped.

Chris was still nowhere to be seen, eventually the
phone rang in my Crash Helmet, we were on the
same road and we were still heading in the same
direction. After a couple of seconds we established
that we would be re-united after the next left hand

bend, after another couple of minutes we agreed
that it would most likely be the service station on
the right and so the chase went on for the next 35
miles. Somehow in the maelstrom of rain and mist
and Inverness traffic Paul and I had overtaken
Chris! This was an absolute miracle, which, were
we not wet and pissed off, would have been cele-
brated and chanted for all to rejoice. As it was we
pulled into what can only be described as the posh-
est service station on the planet and waited. We sat
in the restaurant of this motorway cornucopia
drinking a very pleasant cup of coffee whilst
throngs of Kilted and Tartan clad pensioners stared
and mumbled over their smoked salmon and white
wine lunches. Black leather clearly not considered
'*à la mode*' in this part of town. Intimidated? You
bet we were!

Chris rolled up and we exploited the moment to
recharge our batteries over another cup. The
weather remained filthy so there was no great drive
to push on. This said, good time had been made so
we elected to march on.

14:30 and we were in Edinburgh, the blackened
cloud giving way to bright, brilliant white sunshine.
We fuelled up and peeled off our waterproofs, Paul
lay on a grass verge and started to snooze, in the
sunshine he also started to steam. The weather was
brightening up we felt confident that there might be

some good riding progress ahead. It was clear, however, that the halcyon days of clear roads and sweeping fast bends were over, cars, impatience and the stupidity of drivers when faced with bikes was starting to creep back in. This recognised, we decided to ride as a tight group, the time for independence replaced by a need to work as a team, look out for each other and effectively turn our three bikes into one moving entity. The great thing was that after nearly 1500 miles we could do this remarkably well, from our faltering start we were now a pack, reading each others minds and understanding the tell tail signs, making openings and ensuring that every move created space for the other two riders. This choreographed masterpiece cleared the way for a rapid run to the boarder with England in just two hours.

As we re-entered England we all gave a cheer, it was as though we felt we ought, for myself I was a little sad. Having witnessed some of the most beautiful scenery this country has to offer and changed my entire outlook during the experience, I felt both moved and eternally grateful to this place, for this reason alone I was sad to leave. There were realisations and emotions I did not want to revisit, but they had been prompted by this wonderful place.

Scotland clearly had a dark side and despite the beauty and majesty of its landscapes, I had been

The Ride

moved by the depth of negative emotion this place had triggered. Ardnamurchan, whilst staggering, struck me as a dark secretive environment. Almost certainly a result of where my head was at the time. This must be, after all, the essence of experience; it is surely a combination of *'where you are'* and *'where you are mentally'* that plants the seed of emotion that grows along side a memory, eventually it is always the emotion we remember, far more than the situation itself. At the point of riding across this overwhelming landscape I was in a dark and troubled state of mind, the combination of an angry sky and a troubled mind creating what is probably an inaccurate memory of this astounding place. To have witnessed such beauty and yet come away believing the place harbours monsters is anomalous; I believe the monsters were all in my head, and whilst I am not a spiritual person I am certain the Stag on the beach knew this better than I. It was not until Sutherland and my Liquorice Road that these monsters were banished and I knew the direction I was to take.

As we hammered along the A68 a congregation of wind turbines gave a pious wave, how lucky to have a deity who can prove his existence.

I was deeply sad to leave Scotland at 16:30 on the 20th June 2007 but England was getting me back in a far better frame of mind. This, thanks to a wonderful place that I would undoubtedly re-discover with my family, if they could remember who I was after what seemed like a three year absence. In truth that is exactly what it had been.

We were not separated nor were we living estranged lives, we were all very much in love and driving hard to make life work. But the priorities were fucked, my time with the children was tense and compensatory, my time with Emma always when we were both (or one of us) too tired to communicate. The pursuit of financial gain and stability was deeply impacting the true stability of this family. There was money but this served to smother everything else. I knew this and hid it away in a cave at the back of my mind, every so often I heard it growling but ignored it or occasionally aired it, then forced it back to its lair. *"There has to be a better way"* the mid-life battle cry we so often hear or utter ourselves between friends. *"I want to give it all up and make scones"* is the regular cry of a great friend and regular colleague, but still she goes on giving three hundred %, just to be asked by the corporate machine to apply again for her own job. The truth is the scones would bring her untold riches, and the money, well its amazing how less of it can facilitate happiness. I certainly needed to change what I did and more importantly the way I did it. Of this I was certain, so certain that there was no turning back. The die was cast.

The Ride

As we rolled into England the cheer was quickly silenced by the vision that was a roadside café. We all needed fuel and possibly a Bacon Butty. In we swept. Topped up with fuel and marched on into the café. Being the only customers in the place didn't bother us. It was filled with references to being the 'first' or the 'last' in England. It's always good to find an identity, no matter how tenuous, like the Pub in Worle village in Somerset claiming to be *'The Best Pub in the Worle'*, or Steve Martin in *'The Jerk'* claiming "*I am somebody!*" when his name appeared in the phone book. Like this innocuous little roadside café, not only did it provided a fantastic Bacon Butty and mug of tea (which for most would be enough), but it was the *'first in England'* and it is always good to be the first. I understood the futility of this concept for the first time in my life, and enjoyed the fare all the more for the knowledge. Unfortunately it was not the first for customer service or friendliness, which is perhaps why we were alone.

The Liquorice Road

I shouldn't be too harsh, the Butty was excellent and three bikers in full leathers can seem a little more than intimidating.

Frighteningly I have no memory of the next few miles, the roads, the bends, hazards or indeed anything at all. I remember leaving the *'first'* café in England, one wrong turn when Chris's SatNav tried to take us back to Scotland and absolutely nothing else. This happens to me sometimes, but usually only on familiar journeys. I am walking to the station, arrive and realise that I can't remember the walk, so deep was I in my thoughts. Or driving a regular route, but never on roads I have not previously navigated. Perhaps so at home with the

The Ride

riding of my compatriots, or so 'at one' with the *Wide Glide*. More likely sheer fatigue and the fact that I was now in such a good place mentally that the daydreaming was taking over. I hope I rode well, I have no idea, the lads didn't complain, I didn't invite comment.

Consett was the destination; we arrived at about 18:00 and were directed to a large pub on the outskirts of town. En route Chris pulled into a car park next to a field, it had several tents pitched. Panic set in as Chris looked longingly towards the tents and then back to us, a brief glance between Paul and I, clutches dropped and we were gone. Chris followed; I felt a little guilty, but not enough to turn me into a camper.

The pub stood majestic on the junction of three roads, presiding over a mini roundabout. In the bar stood an extremely jolly, somewhat rotund little lady, she welcomed us with open arms. This woman had, without any doubt, devoted her entire life to the hospitality industry. She loved her customers and knew instinctively what they wanted.

"Boys! Of course I have rooms for you, but first would you like to lock your bikes up more securely for the night?"
"Great, yes please"
"Follow me I'll show you where to put them"

The Liquorice Road

She continued to issue welcome instructions and generally order our existence for the next few minutes, at the end of which we had secured our steeds in their discreet paddock, locked them to the fabric of the building and proceeded to our 'room for three,' been shown around the establishment and had a table booked for dinner in their very own restaurant. After all it was "*curry night*" which she was sure we would love.

This was a perfect example of a Landlady understanding her clientele and doing exactly what was required. She was fantastic, the beer in the bar was well kept, the atmosphere warm and welcoming and the banter started from the minute I entered the bar. Paul was caught on a call and Chris spent a good hour updating the Honda XRV web site with the day's progress. This afforded me the privilege of a quiet pint; I sat outside the pub on a little wooden Carver which presided over the high street in royal fashion. In enjoyed an ice cold pint of Cider, half way into it my phone gently nudged me.

"Hello dad"

My boy has a wonderful way of making me feel close to him on the phone, just in the gentle way he opens the call, the name Dad slightly elongated. We talked about the days riding and the places

The Ride

seen. He told me about his day. A boy had kicked his violin case over, Jo had not responded (9 year old Green belts usually control themselves quite well) a mate had come to his aide however, the aggressor played up more and got violent, Jo then finished the fight. He then got the telling off from the aggressor's mother, who sees her boy through rose tinted specs, don't we all.

"Life's not fair is it Dad"
"How do you mean son"
"I didn't start the fight, I tried to stop it and I got told off"
"You're right son, life isn't fair"
"Did I do the wrong thing?"
"Did you start it?"
"No"
"Did you make it worse"
"No"
"Did you finish it"
"Yes"
"Do you think you did the wrong thing?"
"No, but I got told off"
"Son, I think you did the right thing, but you guys need to learn to get on. Because, for every nice person there is always at least one 'right little Plonker', and as much as you know he needs a slap, it is generally best to leave him alone and lonely".

The Liquorice Road

He chuckled and we moved on to the more interesting subject of what new tricks he has learned on his Heelies.

My daughter joined the call, the energy level soured.
"Hey Dad, where are you?"
No time to answer
"I'm in the Netball team"
"Wow, excel……." No time to finish
"Pop is taking us to the cinema tonight"
"Great what you going to see?"
"I don't know, I'll get mum, Love You bye"

Most of my conversations with Danielle are like this, I actually find them quite stimulating, if a little exhausting.

My conversation with Emma was much more relaxed, warm, tender and very loving. We weren't exchanging anything other than news and views but the manner in which this happened was full of affection. I hinted that we might be able to make it back for Jo's concert on Friday but stopped short of a promise. She vowed to keep it a secret and made me promise I would not rush. In truth I found myself annoyed with the fact that my plans had omitted attending Jo's concert as it was to be his first ever violin performance and having worked hard for the last year it promised to be a squeaky

The Ride

but sublime effort. It turned out that Paul's son was to perform in the same event as a member of the choir. For the first time I was starting to be quietly grateful to Chris for initially reducing the time available to us.

Chris and Paul joined me in the bar. This was an English Pub the way you would draw one. The public bar packed with all manner of folk, carpets, wall coverings and tables had all seen better days. Old timers and regulars strategically placed around the place, on their marks with a stock conversation with whosoever should get too close. The place precisely orchestrated by a matriarchal landlady to generate the perfect English Pub atmosphere. It was all a product of evolution, by the look of some of the guests, regressive evolution, but Darwinian perfection nonetheless. A couple of pints dispensed with and we headed through to the restaurant, more of the same, though less people exposed a stunning English Oak bar, tall pillars and mirrors. Tables and chairs in rich deep varnish, smells of beer replaced by fine food and wine, and a hint of eastern spice in the air. One perfectly formed Australian waitress at he helm. Curry night for £5.00 a head was probably the best value meal all week, and bloody good!

Another beer and I took my leave; the boys continued the tradition of out-drinking me.

The Liquorice Road

The day had yielded another 360 miles, most of it through mist and rain, as a result the scenery between Inverness and Edinburgh might as well not exist, reportedly, a great loss. The riding this day had so numbed the senses that a good portion had escaped memory completely. MP3s and my thoughts kept me company until the day was lifted by the most traditional of English Landladies. I didn't hear the boys return to the room, though I was later serenaded by them both snoring in not so perfect harmony. Of course this was my imagination; neither of them snores, according to them at least.

10

Thursday 21st June 2007
The Longest Day 7
(512 miles to go)

Up and out early, the bikes duly released from their safe refuge and sparked up in the car park. The *Wide Glide*, according to Chris and Paul, responsible for waking the whole of the North East. For the first time on the trip I suspected they were becoming a little bored at the extreme noise it created. The objective for the day was to reach Lowestoft, the easterly most tip of the UK Mainland. We had set this goal along with the stretch objective of then heading inland towards St Ives in Cambridgeshire. This is where the Intercom system for my bike had come from and I was hoping to get it fixed as we were in the area. We had had several conversations and they had been keen when I suggested dropping in. This was a refreshing approach as most organisations I come across generally seem reluctant to make good. Starcom clearly saw this as an opportunity to recover by giving excellent service. That said Consett to Lowestoft and then inland to St Ives

95

seemed a long way off. In addition Paul and I had decided to do our level best to get to the school concert by Friday, at 17:00.

The A1M with all its traffic was the sad but obvious choice, we had wanted to avoid major roads at the outset of the journey and had achieved this in the main, but needs must and we didn't have time to do this part of the country justice. We reluctantly settled for a gruelling, boring slog all the way down the eastern spine of the country. The roads the same as any mind numbing commute. To add insult to injury the mental age of drivers was diminishing with each mile we travelled south. All notions of a fantastic escape to the inner reaches of my mind quickly banished as my compatriots and I laboured to stay upright and safe in the face of unfathomable stupidity. Again we re-grouped and rode as a unit, moving together, making openings and ensuring that nobody was left exposed. The weather, whilst at times threatening, held off. This riding was hard work, not because the roads were difficult but because it was boring and because the traffic was heavy.

The first two fuel stops were sombre affairs, we were all tired and getting pissy with each other. This said we remained civil. All recognised the signs and had too much respect for each other to allow the frustration of the days riding to overflow. We were longing for better riding. Chris, quite rightly suggested that once passed The Wash we should head for some smaller roads, we all agreed.

The Ride

For a time the weather seemed to brighten and as we approached the long overdue left turn from the A1 onto the A17 and the chance to strike out for some better roads, my spirits were beginning to lift. The roads were bound to improve. They didn't, moreover it seemed that the roads had narrowed, just enough to make overtaking, even on a bike, impossible. The next 30 miles took an hour and seemed to sap every last ounce of patience and enthusiasm out of me. Then, as if perfectly choreographed, the skies tore themselves open and down poured another few million gallons. It was 15:30 and we were still 40 miles the wrong side of Norwich. The planned detour was simply not going to happen, the numbers didn't add up. We still had another couple of hours to go, just to get the final compass point. We eventually pulled over and had the conversation that nobody wanted to have, we decided to stay on schedule, cut out the scenic detour and push on to Lowestoft. This decision alone prompted the skies to clear, spirits to lift and the riding to become easier.

East Anglia, compared with the rest of the country is bereft of anything of note; landscape flat, architecture uninspired, roads shite. That said we were nearly there, we had nearly done it. Once past Norwich the entire tenor of the day changed. We were within spitting distance of having completed the Four Compass Points; our goal was within close grasp. The grim riding and mind numbing fatigue educed by the idiots who frequent the A1M and A17 were becoming as much part of the legend of this trip as my Ardnamurchan Stag, the misty

97

The Liquorice Road

Dartmoor morning, Hardnott Pass and my Liquorice Road. The smiles crept back as I cranked up *'No More Heroes'* and powered down the coast road.

Chris' SatNav took over as we got into Lowestoft, once again we were convinced it was playing up as it took us through a run down industrial park, onto a shingle path and into a large concrete car park. We rode around in puzzled circles, surveying the crass miss-spelt graffiti and drifts of litter, used condoms and hypodermic syringes. The realisation was horrific, this was it, this was the treasure we had been seeking, this was the pot of gold at the end of the rainbow. Lowestoft Ness, the eastern most point on the UK mainland is a complete and utter shit hole.

The tour of our beautiful country, this eventful, enlightening voyage of discovery had landed us squarely in the heart of the affluent South East. The one destination on the entire journey which could and should have afforded to make something of this geographical gift it had been blessed with, nothing of the sort, a plaque in the ground and plenty of room for litter, drug paraphernalia and graffiti. The irony of this cold welcome back to 21st century England was not missed, nor was it necessary to discuss it. We were all simply and profoundly disappointed. A photo was taken to prove our attendance and away, before evening and the inevitable arrival of the night breed to re-litter their territory. We gunned out of Lowestoft as though running from the devil himself.

Our escape from East Anglia was quick as it could be and no ride as joyful. As we approached Cambridgeshire the roads improved, the comfort of the Shire counties welcomed us in a shroud of velvet green with free standing homes on sweeping driveways. As negatively as one can view this landscape it was infinitely better that Lowestoft Ness.

St Ives, Cambridgeshire. A pretty paved village/town in the heart of middle England, as unique as The Shire in the heart of Middle Earth. It looked as though nothing could touch this Pleasantville, not time, grime or any unpleasantness at all. We pulled up in the centre of the market ready high street with its ample pavement down the middle of the road. Chris sat dazed by fatigue on the wooden bench. Paul and I marched down to the 'The Au-

The Liquorice Road

Pairs Arms' at the bottom of the street. This beautifully kept establishment was just filling up with its early evening crowd. Still suited and booted the middle management trotted in followed by the 50+ overweight business owners, Gold Rolex, striped shirt white collar and cuffs, pint of the usual, and one for yourself. Comments to the bar maid that no self respecting, politically aware would ever make. Bar maid too good at her job to let it draw a response.

They had rooms, excellent rooms. This was a really friendly place with an excellent team. Despite this we were reluctant to break the news to Chris that we had found accommodation instead the message was to be a good deal crueller.

"Chris"
"Mmm"
"They've got no room"
"Oh"
"But don't worry, they have another pub 25 miles from here, they have booked us in there"
"25 miles?"
"Yeh, come on, lets go"!
"OOOh Kay"

We mounted and proceeded to ride around the one way system, left, left and left again, into the rear car park of the Pub.

*"W****ers"*

The Ride

All smiled and started to unload, the skies opened once more, this time, big heavy raindrops, within seconds we were drenched, well I was, Chris as ever the sensible one had kept his waterproofs on and Paul had locked himself upstairs in the bedroom (inadvertently) and was enjoying a long telephone call with his mother-ship.

Showered and warmed up we hit the pub, pints lined up with intent. So close to the end and with the Four Compass Points complete, tonight was a night for celebration. Whilst quietly rejoicing at the achievement, the feeling of finality was tangible. This was the last complete day we would ride together as Chris would strike south for home and Paul and I would head back toward the mystic South West, Glastonbury Tor and a summer solstice in the rain.

There was only one thing for it, a curry, not a pub curry, a proper one. We were advised that 'Massala Palace' was the best in the area (I suspect it was the only one) we seized the recommendation. If this was the only place in town they had clearly not relaxed for lack of competition. The meal was exceptional, staff attentive and price very reasonable. The tenor of the entire conversation was on what an excellent trip it had been, how dangerous Chris' dispatch riding had become, how slow and nervous my riding was and just how dashed sensible Paul's riding was. All in all we had learnt to ride well together and seen some staggeringly beautiful sights.

The Liquorice Road

I got the impression the boys had also spent time finding their own thoughts, as I had mine. The content of these for them to act on and divulge as they see fit, suffice to say, had they made the kind of decisions I had, change was afoot.

A fantastic curry finished we headed for the pub and a final pint. The day had been amongst the toughest, it was relentlessly boring for the main part, dangerous due to foolish drivers and fiercely disappointing as Lowestoft listed itself as one of the UK's most hugely missed opportunities.

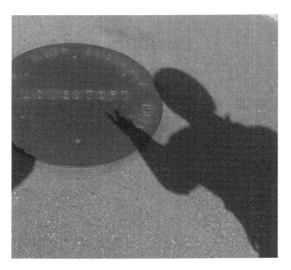

All of this balanced by a great sense of achievement. 336 miles had been munched through; rain, idiots and fierce winds had not stopped us. The job was all but complete.

Friday 22st June 2007
Day 8
(176 miles home)

St Ives might have a great curry house and a wonderful pub, but that same wonderful pub served one
of the most bland breakfasts I have ever had the
misfortune to start a day with. The sausages dry
and flavourless, the bacon thin and dull, eggs over-
cooked, baked beans obviously the budget variety
and so on. It did look good on the plate though. It
wasn't worth complaining as all else had been excellent and we were all too mellow to let this soil
our week.

Having loaded our noble and trusty steeds for a last
time we headed for the headquarters of Starcom
Communications Ltd. Chris and I had fitted this
equipment before the ride to ensure that we could
communicate throughout the journey using Walkie-
Talkies fitted to the bikes. This element of the
equipment had not worked. Unfortunately we had

discovered this problem just before setting out. As such we did not have time to resolve it prior to leaving. As a result we had arranged to call in en-route to fix the problem. 'En-route' had however ended up a 'Fin de route'. This said we encountered an absolutely fabulous bunch of people who could not do enough to help us out. The problems were all fixed and we got on our way. But not before we all said our goodbyes. Chris was going to head straight for the A10 whilst we were going west. Farewells were brief and manly. Chris and I enjoyed another 90 second conversation before our opposite trajectories took us out of radio contact.

Having spent the last week deriding Chris' SatNav system, we were certainly too embarrassed to call him on the phone to tell him that we had gotten so helplessly lost as to add a further 24 miles to our journey. Once back on track we headed for Bedford and on to Milton Keynes, where, just for good measure the skies opened again. Mercilessly beating us into submission on the A34 north of Oxford. Here we stopped at the Little Chef and ordered lunch. Throughout this journey the Little Chef had become our roadside home from home, always there to soothe our tired eyes and add substance or simply a place to unwind. Its perfect familiarity and predictability a joy, the menu that didn't need opening, the buttered toast so perfect that it is a must with every Little Chef creation, even the pancakes and ice cream. Almost as rewarding as a hug from your mum. When you start to think of the Little Chef with this much affection, its time to get home. We waited until the rain had stopped, though why is unclear, as it resumed as soon as we started to ride. We filled up and set out on the last leg. Paul led for most of the way; this was a pure survival technique on my part. I had recently read a statistic which indicated that the majority of motorcycle accidents occur within 5 miles of home or within the last 5% of any journey. Paul was a better and more astute rider than I.

We made it home through constant rain and wind by 15:00. The school concert started at 17:00. Showered and shaved Paul and I greeted each other knowingly at the entrance to the school hall and diverted our attentions to the performances, which were as every primary school performance should be.

Sitting with my wife and daughter and watching my boy was blissful. With the concert over we went to the Golden Phoenix for Crispy Aromatic Duck, drank a bottle of Chablis and talked about the performance. We then moved on to developments at Danielle's school and everything that had happened to them in the last 8 days. Before going to bed I sat down at my laptop and wrote my resignation.

The Liquorice Road

Riding the Four Compass Points of the UK mainland will never be listed as a great expedition, nor will it be hailed as a mammoth feat of endurance or discovery. But it was our achievement. It delivered me at least, a real sense of perspective and clarity.

The Picture Book

Day 2 Ejected from the dank Dartmoor woodland, refreshed by a good night's sleep and on our way to The Lizard. Followed by the only Taxi on Dartmoor.

Day 2 The Lizard, the most Southerly Tip of the UK Mainland, a wild unforgiving place, ravaged by wind and sea, barely enough parking for a Peugeot and a Ford Fiesta, and a Tea Room that had run out of Carrot Cake.

Lured by the scent of Bacon and Eggs the boys beat a hasty retreat, hammering on for a full two minutes before stopping for Breakfast.

By the end of Day two we were back where we started! "Take a walk on the Wild Side".

Day 3. Wales and things were looking up, clear roads, friendly bikers and not a Speed Camera in sight.. Don't be silly, this was Wales.

By the end of Day 3 we were all commenting on how nobody deserves a view like this one, no matter how good they have been.

The Liquorice Road

Day 4. We skirted the lake for a while before heading up to the mountains. These roads were narrow but great fun, dry and very quiet. That was until the Wide Glide arrived.

Hardknott Pass was steep and windy, not ideal for the Harley, Perfect for the Africa Twin and Paul could do practically anything he wanted with the GPZ. Spectacular views and the weather held off.

Chris managed a good smile after clearing the Pass, Paul stayed cool, very cool, bit too cool really.

From the Cumbrian Mountains we powered on the Glasgow and found the A82, without a doubt one of the best motorcycling roads on the planet. Not to mention the view.

A welcome rest as we crossed the Loch, the Pub on the far side taking far too long to come into focus.

The crossing over and the long ride from the Ferry to the Pub complete, we stop for a well earned rest. Potentially a major mistake, sitting down at 17:00 in the afternoon for a pint, in the sun, with that view.

We rode on to Salen and stopped to feed the Midges, what looks like trees in this photograph is a wave of Midges, all female and all starving. All sharing a common goal, to empty three peaceful bikers of every last drop of blood. Little Fuckers!

A wet morning ride to Ardenamurchan, stunning, unsettling, slippery, spectacular.

The Liquorice Road

The Westerly most tip of the UK Mainland; also the quietest place on the planet. It has just dawned on me that there were no birds, not even fat ones.

Heading east, one thing on our minds, Breakfast!!

*The stag patrolled this beach and seized my imagination.
It also made me go very slowly, much to the annoyance
of by compadres.*

*Major traffic problems in Southerland, the local popula-
tion out in the streets, conducting a dirty protest.*

The Liquorice Road

This track (the A897) leading to the Liquorice Road.

Out of the top of Southerland and into the icy cold winds of the North (A836). This was the last blast towards Dunnet Head. We were tired and freezing.

With every mile it got smaller, sorry, colder. People seemed to shuffle along sideways with their heads buried in their sweaters. Walking sideways to battle the constant icy wind.

Dunnet Head, the Northerly most tip of the UK Mainland, the wind like daggers. Three compass points conquered, and the prospect of a night camping at the edge of the world.

117

The Liquorice Road

We found the one available tourist to take a picture and resolved to head South, fast, not stopping until we found a Guest House.

Some roads were less than ideal for the Harley.

118

The Ride

Back down the East Coast road A99, gradually regaining the feeling in my limbs, accelerating past Campsites slowing past B&Bs.

After an entertaining night in Helmsdale (in a B&B) we pushed through some of the worst storms of the trip, the skys only clearing to welcome us home to Blighty. We decided to head for Consett (on the A68) and call it a day.

The Liquorice Road

A long boring and dangerous days riding down the spine of the country (A1 and onto the A17, A47 and finally the A12) delivered us to this beautiful place. Lowestoft Ness, Easterly most point of the UK mainland.

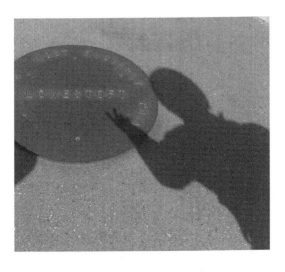

The Ride

Job done!

The Liquorice Road

The Route for all you Anoraks !!

From	To	Road
Bleadon Village	Bridgewater	A38
Bridgewater	Taunton	A38
Taunton	Tiverton	A38
Tiverton	Exeter	A396
Exeter	Princetown	B3212
Princetown	Plymouth	A386
Plymouth	Liskeard	A38
Liskeard	Truro	A390
Truro	Helston	A394
Helston	Lizard	B3083
Helston	Longrock	A394
Longrock	Bodmin	A30
Bodmin	Exeter	A30
Exeter	Bridgewater	M5
Bridgewater	Wick St Lawrence	A38
Wick St Lawrence	Newport (Gwent)	M5/M4
Newport	Abergavenny	A449/A40
Abergavenny	Bronllys	A479
Bronllys	Crossgates	A470/A483
Crossgates	Wrexham	A483
Wrexham	Chester	A483
Chester	Kendal	M56/M6
Kendal	Windermere	A591

The Ride

	Keswick	A593/A595
Keswick	Penrith	A66
Penrith	Glasgow	M6/A74
Glasgow	Crianlarich	A82
Crianlarich	Corran	A82
Corran	Ardgour	Ferry
Ardgour	Salen	A861
Salen	Achosnich	B8007
Achosnich	Ardenamurchan	Track
Ardenamurchan	Achosnich	Track
Achosnich	Salen	B8007
Salen	Lochyside	A861/A830
Lochyside	Inverness	A82
Inverness	Helmsdale	A9
Helmsdale	Golval	A897
Golval	Dunnet Head	A836
Dunnet Head	Helmsdale	A99/A9
Helmsdale	Inverness	A9
Inverness	Edinburgh	A9
Edinburgh	Consett	A68
Consett	Newark-on-Trent	A1
Newark-on-Trent	Kings Lynn	A17
Kings Lynn	Norwich	A47
Norwich	Great Yarmouth	A47
Great Yarmouth	Lowestoft	A12
Lowestoft	Bury St Edmonds	A14
Bury St Edmonds	St Ives	A14
St Ives	Bedford	A14/A1/A421
Bedford	Bicester	A421/A4421

The Liquorice Road

Bicester	Oxford	A34
Oxford	Slough	A420
Slough	Bristol	M4
Bristol	Wick/Bleadon	M5